Mediterranean Diet Tips For Beginners

A Straightforward Guide To Learn Quick And Easy Mouth-Watering Recipes That Busy And Novice Can Cook

Natalie Dorsey

Table of contents

Introduction

About the Mediterranean Diet

The Mediterranean diet is full of never-ending varieties of healthy, fresh, and delicious foods. However, there is more of an emphasis on certain types of foods, nothing is excluded. People who try a Mediterranean diet can enjoy the dishes they love while also learning to appreciate how good the freshest, healthiest foods can be.

Benefits of the Mediterranean Diet

Boosts Your Brain Health: Preserve memory and prevent cognitive decline by following the Mediterranean diet that will limit processed foods, refined bread, and red meats. Have a glass of wine versus hard liquor.

Improves Poor Eyesight: Older individuals suffer from poor eyesight, but in many cases, the Mediterranean diet has provided notable improvement. An Australian Center for Eye Research discovered that the individuals who consumed a minimum of 100 ml (0.42 cup) of olive oil weekly were almost 50% less likely to develop macular degeneration versus those who ate less than one ml each week.

Helps to Reduce the Risk of Heart Disease: The New England Journal of Medicine provided evidence in 2013 from a randomized clinical trial. The trial was implemented in Spain, whereas individuals did not have cardiovascular disease at enrollment but were in the 'high risk' category. The incidence of major cardiovascular events was reduced by the Mediterranean diet that was supplemented with extra-virgin olive oil or nuts. In one study, men who consumed fish in this manner reduced the risk by 23% of death from heart disease.

The Risk of Alzheimer's disease is reduced: In 2018, the journal Neurology studied 70 brain scans of individuals who had no signs of dementia at the onset. They followed the eating patterns in a two-year study resulting in individuals who were on the Med diet had a lesser increase of the depots and reduced energy use - potentially signaling risk for Alzheimer's.

Helps Lessen the Risk of Some Types of Cancer: According to the results of a group study, the diet is associated with a lessened risk of stomach cancer (gastric adenocarcinoma).

Decreases Risks for Type 2 Diabetes: It can help stabilize blood sugar while protecting against type 2 diabetes with its low-carb elements. The Med diet maintains a richness in fiber, which will digest slowly while preventing variances in your blood sugar. It also can help you maintain a healthier weight, which is another trigger for diabetes.

Suggests Improvement for Those with Parkinson's disease: By consuming foods on the Mediterranean diet, you add high levels of antioxidants that can prevent your body from undergoing oxidative stress, which is a damaging process that will attack your cells. The menu plan can reduce your risk factors in half.

Mediterranean Diet Pyramid

The Mediterranean Diet Pyramid is a nutritional guide developed by the World Health Organization, Harvard School of Public Health, and Oldways Preservation Trust in 1993. It is a visual tool that summarizes the Mediterranean diet, suggested eating patterns, and guides how frequently specific mechanisms should be eaten. It allows you to break healthy eating habits and not overfill yourself with too many calories.

Olive oil, fruits, vegetables, whole grains, legumes, beans, nuts & seeds, spices & herbs: These foods form the Mediterranean pyramid base. If you did observe, you would notice that these are mostly from plant sources. You should try and include a few variations of these items into each meal you eat. Olive oil should be the primary fat in cooking your dishes and endeavor to replace any other butter or cooking oil you may have been using to cook.

Fish & seafood: These are essential staples of the Mediterranean diet that should be consumed often as a protein source. You would want to include these in your diet at least two times a week. Try new varieties of fish, either frozen or fresh. Also, incorporate seafood like mussels, crab, and shrimp into your diet. Canned tuna is also great to include on sandwiches or toss in a salad with fresh vegetables.

Cheese, yogurt, eggs & poultry: These ingredients should be consumed in more moderate amounts. Depending on the food, they should be used sparingly throughout the week. Keep in mind that if you are using eggs in baking or cooking, they will also be counted in your weekly limit. You would want to stick to more healthy cheese like Parmesan, ricotta, or feta that you can add a topping or garnish on your dishes.

Red meat & sweets: These items are going to be consumed less frequently. If you are going to eat them, you need to consume only small quantities, most preferably lean meat versions with less fat when possible. Most studies recommend a maximum of 12 to 16 ounces per month. To add more variety to your diet, you can still have red meat occasionally, but you would want to reduce how often you have it.

Water: The Mediterranean diet encourages you to stay hydrated at all times. It means drinking more water than your daily intake. The Institute of Medicine recommends a total of 9 cups each day for women and 13 cups for men. For pregnant or breastfeeding women, the number should be increased.

Wine: Moderate consumption of wine with meals is encouraged on the Mediterranean diet. Studies shown that moderate consumption of alcohol can reduce the risk of heart disease. That can mean about 1 glass per day for women. Men tend to have higher body mass so that they can consume 1 to 2 drinks. Please keep in mind what your doctor would recommend regarding wine consumption based on your health and family history.

10 Tips for Success

The healthy Mediterranean way of life is about eating balanced foods rich in vitamins, minerals, antioxidants, and healthy fatty acids. However, the Mediterranean diet is just one aspect of it. The Mediterranean way of life calls for regular physical exercise, plenty of rest, healthy social interaction, and fun. Balancing all these aspects was the secret of the excellent health of the Mediterranean folk back in the day. However, only the Mediterranean diet is the primary focus of this book, and we will spend most of our time talking about just that.

1. Eat Healthy Fats

The Mediterranean diet is not low-fat diet at all, but the fat included in this diet is considered healthy for the body, and the heart in particular. Remember: not all fats are created equal. Certain kinds of fats are beneficial, while others do more harm than good. Monosaturated fats and polyunsaturated omega-3 fatty acids, for example, are considered healthy. Omega-6 polyunsaturated fatty acids and saturated fats are unhealthy, and these harmful fats are primarily present in most of the typical food worldwide.

2. Consume Dairy in Moderation

We all love cheese. Dairy products are delicious, nutritious, and excellent sources of calcium and should be consumed in moderation if you're following the Mediterranean diet. It is usually a good idea to drink two to three servings of full-fat dairy products in a single day, where one serving can mean an 8-ounce glass of milk, or an ounce of cheese or 8 ounces of yogurt.

3. Consume Tons of Plant-Based Foods

As we saw in the pyramid, fruits, vegetables, legumes, and whole grains form the basis of the Mediterranean diet. So, it is a good idea to eat five to ten servings of these in a single day, depending on your appetite. Eat as many as you want, but don't overeat. Plant-based foods are naturally low in calories and high in fiber and nutrients. Fresh, unprocessed plants are best, so always be on the lookout for the best sources of these around you!

4. Spice Things Up with Fresh Spices and Herbs

Fresh herbs and spices make most of the recipes insanely delicious while also providing health benefits. If you already use these in your daily cooking, more power to you! If not, we got you covered!

5. Consume Seafood Weekly and Meat Monthly

As we've talked about before, one benefit of living close to the sea is easy access to seafood. However, seafood holds a lower priority than plant-based foods in the Mediterranean diet and should be consumed in moderation. If you're a vegetarian, consider taking fish oil supplements to get those omega-3 fatty acids into your system.

Consume Meat Monthly: Red meat used to be a luxury for the Mediterranean people back in the day. Although not completely off-limits, you should try and reduce your red-meat intake as much as possible. If you love red meat, consider consuming it no more than two times per month. And even when you eat it, make sure the serving size of the meat in the dish is small (two to three-ounce serving). The main reason to limit meat intake is to limit the number of unhealthy fats going into your system. As we talked before, saturated fats and omega-6 fatty acids are not suitable for health, but unfortunately, red meat contains significant quantities. As a beef lover myself, I eat a two-ounce serving of it per month, and when I do eat it, I make sure there are lots of vegetables on the side to satiate my hunger.

Drink Wine! Love wine? Well, it is your lucky day. Drinking 1 glass of wine along with your meal at dinner is a common practice in the Mediterranean regions. Red wine is especially useful for the heart and it is a good idea to consume 1 glass of red wine twice in 1 week. Excess of everything is bad, and wine is no exception so keep it in check. Also, if you're already suffering from health conditions, it is a good idea to check with your doctor before introducing wine to your daily diet.

6. Work Your Body

Now you don't have to hit the gym like a maniac to work your body. Walking to your destination instead of driving, taking the stairs instead of the lift, or kneading your dough can all get the job done. So, be creative and work your body when you can. Better yet, play a sport or just hit the gym like a maniac. You don't have to, as I said at the start, but it will help… a lot.

7. Enjoy a Big Lunch

Lunch was usually the meal of the day when the Mediterranean residents sat with their families and took their time enjoying a big meal. This strengthens social bonds and relaxes the mind during the most stressful time of the day, when you're just halfway done with your work, probably.

8. Have Fun with Friends and Family

Just by spending time and doing something fun with your loved ones is great for de-stressing. Today, we don't understand the importance of this, and people feel lonely, and in some cases, even depressed. Just doing this one thing has the power to solve a huge chunk of the problems our modern society faces.

9. Be Passionate

The Mediterranean people are passionate folk. Living on or close to sun-kissed coasts, their passion for life is naturally high. Being passionate about something in life can take you a long way towards health and wellness.

10. Planning Your Meals

If you're a beginner and have not yet made the switch to the Mediterranean diet, you will need to identify what changes you need to make to your current diet to make it match closely with the Mediterranean diet. In time, the Mediterranean diet will come to you naturally, but to start, you will need to plan. You will need to plan your portion sizes, and how often you eat certain foods. The changes are small but will benefit you in the long run.

Appetizer and Snack Recipes

1. Cheesy Caprese Salad Skewers

Preparation Time: 15 minutes

Cooking Time: 0 minute

Serving: 10

Size/ Portion: 2 skewers

Ingredients:

- 8-oz cherry tomatoes, sliced in half
- A handful of fresh basil leaves, rinsed and drained
- 1-lb fresh mozzarella, cut into bite-sized slices
- Balsamic vinegar Extra virgin olive oil
- Freshly ground black pepper

Directions:

1. Sandwich a folded basil leaf and mozzarella cheese between the halves of tomato onto a toothpick.

2. Drizzle with olive oil and balsamic vinegar each skewer. To serve, sprinkle with freshly ground black pepper.

Nutrition:

94 Calories

3.7g Fats

2.1g Protein

2. Leafy Lacinato Tuscan Treat

Preparation Time: 10 minutes

Cooking Time: 0 minute

Serving: 1

Size/ Portion: 3 wraps

Ingredients:

- 1-tsp Dijon mustard
- 1-tbsp light mayonnaise
- 3-pcs medium-sized Lacinato kale leaves
- 3-oz. cooked chicken breast, thinly sliced
- 6-bulbs red onion, thinly sliced
- 1-pc apple, cut into 9-slices

Directions:

1. Mix the mustard and mayonnaise until fully combined.

2. Spread the mixture generously on each of the kale leaves. Top each leaf with 1-oz. chicken slices, 3-apple slices, and 2-red onion slices. Roll each kale leaf into a wrap.

Nutrition:

370 Calories

14g Fats

29g Protein

3. Greek Guacamole Hybrid Hummus

Preparation Time: 10 minutes

Cooking Time: 0 minute

Serving: 1

Size/ Portion: 1-unit

Ingredients:

- 1-15 oz. canned chickpeas
- 1-pc ripe avocado
- ¼-cup tahini paste
- 1-cup fresh cilantro leaves
- ¼-cup lemon juice
- 1-tsp ground cumin
- ¼-cup extra-virgin olive oil
- 1-clove garlic
- ½ tsp salt

Directions:

1. Drain the chickpeas and reserve 2-tablespoons of the liquid. Pour the reserved liquid in your food processor and add in the drained chickpeas.

2. Add the avocado, tahini, cilantro, lemon juice, cumin, oil, garlic, and salt. Puree the mixture into a smooth consistency.

3. Serve with pita chips, veggie chips, or crudités.

Nutrition:

156 Calories 12g Fats 3g Protein

Breakfast Recipes

4. Avocado and Apple Smoothie

Preparation Time: 6 minutes

Cooking Time: 0 minutes

Serving: 2

Size/ Portion: 1 glass

Ingredients

- 3 c. spinach
- 1 cored green apple, chopped
- 1 pitted avocado, peeled and chopped
- 3 tbsps. chia seeds
- 1 tsp. honey
- 1 frozen banana, peeled 2 c. coconut water

Directions:

1. Using your blender, add in all the ingredients.

2. Process well for 5 minutes to obtain a smooth consistency and serve in glasses.

Nutrition

208 Calories

10.1g Fat

2.1g Protein

5. Mini Frittatas

Preparation Time: 9 minutes

Cooking Time: 20 minutes

Serving: 8

Size/ Portion: 2 frittatas

Ingredients:

- 1 chopped yellow onion
- 1 c. grated parmesan
- 1 chopped yellow bell pepper
- 1 chopped red bell pepper
- 1 chopped zucchini
- Salt and black pepper
- A drizzle of olive oil
- 8 whisked eggs
- 2 tbsps. chopped chives

Directions:

1. Set a pan over medium-high heat. Add in oil to warm. Stir in all ingredients except chives and eggs. Sauté for around 5 minutes.
2. Put the eggs on a muffin pan and top by the chives.
3. Set oven to 350 °F. Place the muffin pan into the oven to bake for about 10 minutes.
4. Serve the eggs on a plate with sautéed vegetables.

Nutrition

55 Calories

3g Fat

4.2g Protein

6. Sun-Dried Tomatoes Oatmeal

Preparation Time: 4 minutes

Cooking Time: 20 minutes

Serving: 4

Size/ Portion: 1 cup

Ingredients:

- 3 c. water
- 1 c. almond milk
- 1 tbsp. olive oil
- 1 c. steel-cut oats
- ¼ c. chopped tomatoes, sun-dried
- A pinch of red pepper flakes

Directions:

1. Using a pan, add water and milk to mix. Set on medium heat and allow to boil.

2. Set up another pan on medium-high heat. Warm oil and add oats to cook for 2 minutes. Transfer to the first pan plus tomatoes then stir. Let simmer for approximately 20 minutes.

3. Set in serving bowls and top with red pepper flakes. Enjoy.

Nutrition

170 Calories

17.8g Fat

1.5g Protein

7. Mushrooms and Turkey Breakfast

Preparation time: 10 minutes

Cooking time: 1 hour and 5 minutes

Servings: 12

Ingredients:

- 8 ounces whole-wheat bread, cubed
- 12 ounces turkey sausage, chopped
- 2 cups fat-free milk
- 5 ounces low-fat cheddar, shredded
- 3 eggs
- ½ cup green onions, chopped
- 1 cup mushrooms, chopped
- ½ teaspoon sweet paprika
- A pinch of black pepper
- 2 tablespoons low-fat parmesan, grated

Directions:

1. Put the bread cubes on a prepared lined baking sheet, bake at 400 °F for 8 minutes. Meanwhile, heat a pan over medium-high heat, add turkey sausage, stir, and brown for 7 minutes.
2. In a bowl, combine the milk with the cheddar, eggs, parmesan, black pepper, and paprika and whisk well.
3. Add mushrooms, sausage, bread cubes, and green onions stir, pour into a baking dish, bake at 350 degrees F within 50 minutes. 5. Slice, divide between plates and serve for breakfast.

Nutrition:

Calories: 88

Carbs: 1g

Fat: 9g

Protein: 1g

Sodium: 74 mg

8. Mushrooms and Cheese Omelet

Preparation time: 10 minutes

Cooking time: 15 minutes

Servings: 4

Ingredients:

- 2 tablespoons olive oil A pinch of black pepper
- 3 ounces mushrooms, sliced
- 1 cup baby spinach, chopped
- 3 eggs, whisked
- 2 tablespoons low-fat cheese, grated
- 1 small avocado, peeled, pitted, and cubed
- 1 tablespoons parsley, chopped

Directions:

1. Add mushrooms, stir, cook them for 5 minutes and transfer to a bowl on a heated pan with the oil over medium-high heat.

2. Heat-up the same pan over medium-high heat, add eggs and black pepper, spread into the pan, cook within 7 minutes, and transfer to a plate.

3. Spread mushrooms, spinach, avocado, and cheese on half of the omelet, fold the other half over this mix, sprinkle parsley on top, and serve.

Nutrition:

Calories: 136

Carbs: 5g

Fat: 5g

Protein: 16g

Sodium: 192 mg

9. Egg White Breakfast Mix

Preparation time: 10 minutes

Cooking time: 10 minutes

Servings: 4

Ingredients:

- 1 yellow onion, chopped
- 3 plum tomatoes, chopped
- 10 ounces spinach, chopped
- A pinch of black pepper
- 2 tablespoons water
- 12 egg whites
- Cooking spray

Directions:

1. Mix the egg whites with water and pepper in a bowl. Grease a pan with cooking spray, heat up over medium heat, add ¼ of the egg whites, spread into the pan, and cook for 2 minutes.

2. Spoon ¼ of the spinach, tomatoes, and onion, fold, and add to a plate. 4. Serve for breakfast. Enjoy!

Nutrition:

Calories: 31

Carbs: 0g

Fat: 2g

Protein: 3g

Sodium: 55 mg

Main Dish Recipes

10. Slow Cooked Daube Provencal

Preparation Time 15 minutes

Cooking Time: 4–8 hours

Serving: 8–10

Size/ Portion: ½ lb.

Ingredients:

- 1 tablespoon olive oil
- 10 garlic cloves, minced
- 2 pounds boneless chuck roast
- 1½ teaspoons salt
- ½ teaspoon black pepper
- 1 cup dry red wine
- 2 cups carrots, chopped
- 1½ cups onion, chopped

- ½ cup beef broth
- 1 (14-ounce) can diced tomatoes
- 1 tablespoon tomato paste
- 1 teaspoon fresh rosemary, chopped
- 1 teaspoon fresh thyme, chopped
- ½ teaspoon orange zest, grated
- ½ teaspoon ground cinnamon
- ¼ teaspoon ground cloves
- 1 bay leaf

Directions:

1. Preheat skillet and then add the olive oil. Cook minced garlic and onions
2. Add the cubed meat, salt, and pepper and cook until the meat has browned.
3. Transfer the meat to the slow cooker.

4. Put beef broth to the skillet and let simmer for about 3 minutes to deglaze the pan, then pour into slow cooker over the meat.
5. Add the rest of the ingredients to the slow cooker and stir well to combine.
6. Set your slow cooker to low and cook for 8 hours, or set to high and cook for 4 hours.
7. Serve with a side of egg noodles, rice or some crusty Italian bread.

Nutrition:

547 Calories

30.5g fat

45.2g protein

11. Osso Bucco

Preparation Time 30 minutes

Cooking Time 8 hours

Serving: 2–4

Size/ Portion: 1 piece

Ingredients:

- 4 beef shanks or veal shanks 1 teaspoon sea salt
- ½ teaspoon ground black pepper
- 3 tablespoons whole wheat flour
- 1–2 tablespoons olive oil
- 2 medium onions, diced
- 2 medium carrots, diced
- 2 celery stalks, diced
- 4 garlic cloves, minced
- 1 (14-ounce) can diced tomatoes

- 2 teaspoons dried thyme leaves
- ½ cup beef or vegetable stock

Directions:

1. Season the shanks on both sides, then dip in the flour to coat.
2. Heat a large skillet over high heat. Add the olive oil. When the oil is hot, add the shanks and brown evenly on both sides. When browned, transfer to the slow cooker.
3. Pour the stock into the skillet and let simmer for 3–5 minutes while stirring to deglaze the pan.
4. Add the rest of the ingredients to the slow cooker and pour the stock from the skillet over the top.
5. Click slow cooker to low and cook for 8 hours.
6. Serve the Osso Bucco over quinoa, brown rice, or even cauliflower rice.

Nutrition

589 Calories 21.3g fat 74.7g protein

12. Slow Cooker Beef Bourguignon

Preparation Time 5 minutes

Cooking Time 6–8 hours

Serving: 6–8

Size/ Portion: 2 cups

Ingredients:

- 1 tablespoon extra-virgin olive oil 6 ounces bacon
- 3 pounds beef brisket 1 large carrot
- 1 large white onion 6 cloves garlic
- ½ teaspoon coarse salt ½ teaspoon pepper
- 2 tablespoons whole wheat 12 small pearl onions
- 3 cups red wine 2 cups beef stock
- 2 tablespoons tomato paste
- 1 beef bouillon cube
- 1 teaspoon fresh thyme

- 2 tablespoons fresh parsley
- 2 bay leaves 2 tablespoons butter
- 1-pound mushrooms

Directions:

1. Preheat skillet over medium-high heat, pour olive oil. When the oil has heated, cook the bacon until it is crisp, then place it in your slow cooker. Save the bacon fat in the skillet.
2. Dry the beef with a paper towel and cook it in the same skillet with the bacon fat until all sides have the same brown coloring.
3. Transfer to the slow cooker.
4. Add the onions and carrots to the slow cooker and season with the salt and pepper. Stir to combine the ingredients and make sure everything is seasoned.
5. Pour the red wine into the skillet and simmer for 4–5 minutes to deglaze the pan, then whisk in the flour, stirring until smooth.
6. When the liquid has thickened, pour it into the slow cooker and stir to coat everything with the wine mixture. Add the tomato

paste, bouillon cube, thyme, parsley, 4 cloves of garlic, and bay leaf.

7. Set your slow cooker to high and cook for 6 hours, or set to low and cook for 8 hours.
8. Before serving, melt the butter in a skillet over medium heat. When the oil is hot, add the remaining 2 cloves of garlic and cook for about 1 minute before adding the mushrooms.
9. Cook the mushrooms until soft, then add to the slow cooker and mix to combine.
10. Serve with mashed potatoes, rice or noodles.

Nutrition

672 Calories

32g fat

56g protein

Side Recipes

13. Raisin Rice Pilaf

Preparation Time: 13 minutes

Cooking Time: 8 minutes

Serving: 5

Size/ Portion: 2 cups

Ingredients:

- 1 tablespoon olive oil
- 1 teaspoon cumin
- 1 cup onion, chopped
- ½ cup carrot, shredded
- ½ teaspoon cinnamon
- 2 cups instant brown rice
- 1 ¾ cup orange juice
- 1 cup golden raisins

- ¼ cup water
- ½ cup pistachios, shelled
- fresh chives, chopped for garnish

Directions:

1. Place a medium saucepan over medium-high heat before adding in your oil. Add n your onion, and stir often so it doesn't burn. Cook for about five minutes and then add in your cumin, cinnamon and carrot. Cook for about another minute.
2. Add in your orange juice, water and rice. Boil before covering your saucepan. Turn the heat down to medium-low and then allow it to simmer for six to seven minutes.
3. Stir in your pistachios, chives and raisins. Serve warm.

Nutrition:

320 Calories 6g Protein 7g Fat

14. Lebanese Delight

Preparation Time: 7 minutes

Cooking Time: 25 minutes Serving: 5

Size/ Portion: 2 ounces

Ingredients:

- 1 tablespoon olive oil
- 1 cup vermicelli
- 3 cups cabbage, shredded
- 3 cups vegetable broth, low sodium
- ½ cup water
- 1 cup instant brown rice
- ¼ teaspoon sea salt, fine
- 2 cloves garlic
- ¼ teaspoon crushed red pepper
- ½ cup cilantro fresh & chopped lemon slices to garnish

Directions:

1. Get out a saucepan and then place it over medium-high heat. Add in your oil and once it's hot you will need to add in your pasta. Cook for three minutes or until your pasta is toasted. You will have to stir often in order to keep it from burning.

2. Ad in your cabbage, cooking for another four minutes. Continue to stir often.

3. Add in your water and rice. Season with salt, red pepper and garlic before bringing it all to a boil over high heat. Stir, and then cover. Once it's covered turn the heat down to medium-low. Allow it all to simmer for ten minutes.

4. Remove the pan from the burner and then allow it to sit without lifting the lid for five minutes. Take the garlic cloves out and then mash them using a fork. Place them back in, and stir them into the rice. Stir in your cilantro as well and serve warm. Garnish with lemon wedges if desired.

Nutrition:

259 Calories 7g Protein 4g Fat

15. Butter Corn

Preparation time: 10 minutes Cooking time: 4 hours

Servings: 12

Ingredients:

- 20 ounces fat-free cream cheese 10 cups corn
- ½ cup low-fat butter ½ cup fat-free milk
- A pinch of black pepper 2 tablespoons green onions, chopped

Directions:

1. In your slow cooker, mix the corn with cream cheese, milk, butter, black pepper, and onions, cook on Low within 4 hours. Toss one more time, divide between plates and serve as a side dish.

Nutrition:

Calories 279 Fat 18g Cholesterol 52mg

Sodium 165mg Carbohydrate 26g

Fiber 3.5g Sugars 4.8g Protein 8.1g

16. Stevia Peas with Marjoram

Preparation time: 10 minutes

Cooking time: 5 hours

Servings: 12

Ingredients:

- 1-pound carrots, sliced
- 1 yellow onion, chopped
- 16 ounces peas
- 2 tablespoons stevia
- 2 tablespoons olive oil
- 4 garlic cloves, minced ¼ cup of water
- 1 teaspoon marjoram, dried A pinch of white pepper

Directions:

1. In your slow cooker, mix the carrots with water, onion, oil, stevia, garlic, marjoram, white pepper, peas, toss, cover, and

cook on High for 5 hours. Divide between plates and serve as a side dish.

Nutrition:

Calories 71

Fat 2.5g

Sodium 29mg

Carbohydrate 12.1g

Fiber 3.1g

Sugars 4.4g

Protein 2.5g

Potassium 231mg

17. Pilaf with Bella Mushrooms

Preparation time: 10 minutes Cooking time: 3 hours

Servings: 6

Ingredients:

- 1 cup wild rice 6 green onions, chopped
- ½ pound baby Bella mushrooms 2 cups of water
- 2 tablespoons olive oil 2 garlic cloves, minced

Directions:

1. In your slow cooker, mix the rice with garlic, onions, oil, mushrooms, water, toss, cover, and cook on Low for 3 hours. Stir the pilaf one more time, divide between plates and serve.

Nutrition:

Calories 151 Fat 5.1g

Sodium 9mg Carbohydrate 23.3g

Fiber 2.6g Sugars 1.7g

Protein 5.2g

Seafood Recipes

18. Fish Steamed in Parchment with Veggies

Preparation Time: 25 minutes

Cooking Time: 20 minutes

Serving: 4

Size/ portion: 2 ounces

Ingredients:

- Juice of 2 lemons
- 4 tablespoons extra-virgin olive oil
- 2 teaspoons sea salt
- 1 teaspoon freshly ground black pepper
- 4 (6- to 8-ounce) fish fillets
- ½ pound tomatoes, chopped
- ½ cup chopped scallion
- ¼ cup chopped Kalamata olives

- 1 tablespoon capers, drained
- ¼ cup white wine vinegar
- 2 garlic cloves, minced
- 1 fennel bulb

Direction

1. Preheat the oven to 375 °F.
2. Scourge lemon juice, 2 tablespoons of olive oil, salt, and pepper.
3. Add the fish and marinate in the refrigerator for 10 minutes.
4. In a medium bowl, combine the tomatoes, scallion, olives, capers, vinegar, remaining 2 tablespoons of olive oil, and garlic.
5. Fold 4 (12-by-16-inch) pieces of parchment paper in half and cut out a half heart shape, keeping as much of the parchment as possible. Unfold the hearts and place ¼ of the fennel close to the center crease to make a bed for the fish. Top with 1 fish fillet and ¼ of the tomato mixture.
6. Fold the parchment back over the fish and, starting at the bottom end, start folding the edges, overlapping to seal the packet. Bake for 20 minutes.

Nutrition:

277 Calories

16g Fat

27g Protein

19. Swordfish Souvlaki

Preparation Time: 25 minutes

Cooking Time: 10 minutes

Serving: 4

Size/ portion: ½ lb.

Ingredients:

- ½ cup freshly squeezed lemon juice
- ½ cup extra-virgin olive oil
- 1 teaspoon kosher salt
- 1 teaspoon freshly ground black pepper
- 1 teaspoon dried Greek oregano
- 2 pounds swordfish steaks 8 ounces cherry tomatoes
- 1 red onion, quartered

Directions:

1. Scourge lemon juice, olive oil, salt, pepper, and oregano.

2. Add the fish and marinate in the refrigerator for 10 to 15 minutes.
3. Heat a grill to medium-high heat.
4. Skewer the swordfish, tomatoes, and red onion, alternating 1 to 2 pieces of fish for each tomato and onion quarter. Grill the kebabs for 10 minutes.
5. Alternatively, broil the skewers carefully for 3 to 5 minutes per side, checking frequently.
6. Serve with a squeeze of lemon and Avocado Skordalia / Avocado Garlic Spread.

Nutrition:

493 Calories

34g Fat

42g Protein

Vegetable Recipes

20. Spanish Green Beans

Preparation Time: 10 minutes

Cooking Time: 20 minutes

Serving: 4

Size/ Portion: 1 cup

Ingredients:

- ¼ cup extra-virgin olive oil
- 1 large onion, chopped 4 cloves garlic, finely chopped
- 1-pound green beans ½ teaspoons salt, divided
- 1 (15-ounce) can diced tomatoes
- ½ teaspoon freshly ground black pepper

Directions:

1. Position large pot over medium heat, cook olive oil, onion, and garlic.

2. Cut the green beans into 2-inch pieces.

3. Add the green beans and 1 teaspoon of salt to the pot and toss everything together; cook for 3 minutes.

4. Add the diced tomatoes, remaining ½ teaspoon of salt, and black pepper to the pot; continue to cook for another 12 minutes, stirring occasionally.

5. Serve warm.

Nutrition:

200 Calories

4g Protein

14g Fat

21. Rustic Cauliflower and Carrot Hash

Preparation Time: 10 minutes

Cooking Time: 10 minutes

Serving: 4

Size/ Portion: 2 ounces

Ingredients:

- 3 tablespoons extra-virgin olive oil
- 1 large onion
- 1 tablespoon garlic
- 2 cups carrots
- 4 cups cauliflower pieces
- 1 teaspoon salt ½ teaspoon ground cumin

Directions:

1. Preheat a pan over medium heat, cook the olive oil, onion, garlic, and carrots for 3 minutes.

2. Cut the cauliflower into 1-inch or bite-size pieces. Add the cauliflower, salt, and cumin to the skillet and toss to combine with the carrots and onions.

3. Cover and cook for 3 minutes.

4. Toss the vegetables and continue to cook for 4 minutes.

5. Serve warm.

Nutrition:

159 Calories

3g Protein

11g Fat

22. Roasted Brussels Sprouts

Preparation time: 5 minutes

Cooking time: 20 minutes

Servings: 4

Ingredients:

- 1½ pounds Brussels sprouts, trimmed and halved
- 2 tablespoons olive oil
- ¼ teaspoon salt
- ½ teaspoon freshly ground black pepper

Directions:

1. Preheat the oven to 400 °F. Combine the Brussels sprouts and olive oil in a large mixing bowl and toss until they are evenly coated.
2. Turn the Brussels sprouts out onto a large baking sheet and flip them over, so they are cut-side down with the flat part touching the baking sheet. Sprinkle with salt and pepper.

3. Bake within 20 to 30 minutes or until the Brussels sprouts are lightly charred and crisp on the outside and toasted on the bottom. The outer leaves will be extra dark, too. Serve immediately.

Nutrition:

Calories: 134

Fat: 8g

Sodium: 189mg

Carbohydrate: 15g

Protein: 6g

23. Broccoli with Garlic and Lemon

Preparation time: 2 minutes

Cooking time: 4 minutes

Servings: 4

Ingredients:

- 1 cup of water
- 4 cups broccoli florets
- 1 teaspoon olive oil
- 1 tablespoon minced garlic
- 1 teaspoon lemon zest
- Salt
- Freshly ground black pepper

Directions:

1. Put the broccoli in the boiling water in a small saucepan and cook within 2 to 3 minutes. The broccoli should retain its bright-green color. Drain the water from the broccoli.

2. Put the olive oil in a small sauté pan over medium-high heat. Add the garlic and sauté for 30 seconds. Put the broccoli, lemon zest, salt, plus pepper. Combine well and serve.

Nutrition:

Calories: 38g

Fat: 1g

Sodium: 24mg

Carbohydrate: 5g

Protein: 3g

Soup and Stew Recipes

24. Cauliflower Soup

Preparation Time: 9 minutes

Cooking Time: 40 minutes

Serving: 8

Size/ portion: 1 cup

Ingredients:

- 1 large onion finely cut
- 1 medium head cauliflower
- 2-3 garlic cloves, crushed 3 cups water
- ½ cup whole cream 4 tbsp olive oil

Directions:

1. Cook olive oil in a large pot over medium heat and sauté the onion, cauliflower and garlic. Stir in the water and bring the soup to a boil.

2. Reduce heat, cover, and simmer for 40 minutes. Remove the soup from heat add the cream and blend in a blender. Season with salt and pepper.

Nutrition:

221 Calories

19g Fat

8g Protein

25. Moroccan Pumpkin Soup

Preparation Time: 7 minutes

Cooking Time: 54 minutes

Serving: 6

Size/ Portion: 1 cup

Ingredients:

- 1 leek, white part only
- 3 cloves garlic
- ½ tsp ground ginger
- ½ tsp ground cinnamon
- ½ tsp ground cumin
- 2 carrots
- 2 lb. pumpkin
- 1/3 cup chickpeas
- 5 tbsp olive oil

- juice of ½ lemon

Directions:

1. Heat oil in a large saucepan and sauté leek, garlic and 2 teaspoons of salt, stirring occasionally, until soft. Add cinnamon, ginger and cumin and stir. Add in carrots, pumpkin and chickpeas. Stir to combine.
2. Add 5 cups of water and bring the soup to the boil, then reduce heat and simmer for 50 minutes.
3. Pullout from heat, add lemon juice and blend the soup. Heat again over low heat for 4-5 minutes. Serve topped with parsley sprigs.

Nutrition:

241Calories

21g Fat

4g Protein

26. Black Bean Soup

Preparation time: 15 minutes

Cooking time: 8 hours

Servings: 6

Ingredients:

- 1-pound dried black beans, soaked overnight and rinsed
- 1 onion, chopped
- 1 carrot, peeled and chopped
- 2 jalapeño peppers, seeded and diced
- 6 cups Vegetable Broth or store-bought
- 1 teaspoon ground cumin
- 1 teaspoon ground coriander
- 1 teaspoon chili powder
- ½ teaspoon ground chipotle pepper
- ½ teaspoon of sea salt

- ¼ teaspoon freshly ground black pepper
- Pinch cayenne pepper
- ¼ cup fat-free sour cream, for garnish (optional)
- ¼ cup grated low-fat Cheddar cheese, for garnish (optional)

Directions:

1. In your slow cooker, combine all the fixing listed, then cook on low for 8 hours. If you'd like, mash the beans with a potato masher, or purée using an immersion blender, blender, or food processor. Serve topped with the optional garnishes, if desired.

Nutrition:

Calories: 320

Fat: 3g

Carbohydrates: 57g

Fiber: 13g

Protein: 18g

Sodium: 430 mg

27. Chickpea & Kale Soup

Preparation time: 15 minutes

Cooking time: 9 hours

Servings: 6

Ingredients:

- 1 summer squash, quartered lengthwise and sliced crosswise
- 1 zucchini, quartered lengthwise and sliced crosswise
- 2 cups cooked chickpeas, rinsed
- 1 cup uncooked quinoa
- 2 cans diced tomatoes, with their juice
- 5 cups Vegetable Broth, Poultry Broth, or store-bought
- 1 teaspoon garlic powder
- 1 teaspoon onion powder
- 1 teaspoon dried thyme
- ½ teaspoon of sea salt

- 2 cups chopped kale leaves

Directions:

1. In your slow cooker, combine the summer squash, zucchini, chickpeas, quinoa, tomatoes (with their juice), broth, garlic powder, onion powder, thyme, and salt. Cover and cook on low within 8 hours. Stir in the kale. Cover and cook on low for 1 more hour.

Nutrition:

Calories: 221

Fat: 3g

Carbohydrates: 40g

Fiber: 7g

Protein: 10g

Sodium: 124 mg

Vegetarian Recipes

28. Tabbouleh

Preparation Time: 15 minutes

Cooking Time: 5 minutes

Serving: 6

Size/ Portion: 2 cups

Ingredients:

- 4 tablespoons olive oil
- 4 cups riced cauliflower
- 3 garlic cloves
- ½ large cucumber
- ½ cup Italian parsley uice of 1 lemon
- 2 tablespoons red onion
- ½ cup mint leaves, chopped
- ½ cup pitted Kalamata olives

- 1 cup cherry tomatoes
- 2 cups baby arugula
- 2 medium avocados

Directions:

1. Warm 2 tablespoons olive oil in a nonstick skillet over medium-high heat.
2. Add the rice cauliflower, garlic, salt, and black pepper to the skillet and sauté for 3 minutes or until fragrant. Transfer them to a large bowl.
3. Add the cucumber, parsley, lemon juice, red onion, mint, olives, and remaining olive oil to the bowl. Toss to combine well. Reserve the bowl in the refrigerator for at least 30 minutes.
4. Remove the bowl from the refrigerator. Add the cherry tomatoes, arugula, avocado to the bowl. Sprinkle with salt and black pepper, and toss to combine well. Serve chilled.

Nutrition:

198 calories 17.5g fat 4.2g protein

Salad Recipes

29. Roasted Broccoli Salad

Preparation Time: 9 minutes

Cooking Time: 17 minutes

Serving: 4

Size/ portion: 2 cups

Ingredients:

- 1 lb. broccoli
- 3 tablespoons olive oil, divided
- 1-pint cherry tomatoes
- 1 ½ teaspoons honey
- 3 cups cubed bread, whole grain
- 1 tablespoon balsamic vinegar
- ½ teaspoon black pepper
- ¼ teaspoon sea salt, fine

- grated parmesan for serving

Directions:

1. Set oven to 450 °F, and then place rimmed baking sheet.
2. Drizzle your broccoli with a tablespoon of oil, and toss to coat.
3. Take out from oven, and spoon the broccoli. Leave oil at bottom of the bowl and add in your tomatoes, toss to coat, then mix tomatoes with a tablespoon of honey. place on the same baking sheet.
4. Roast for fifteen minutes, and stir halfway through your cooking time.
5. Add in your bread, and then roast for three more minutes.
6. Whisk two tablespoons of oil, vinegar, and remaining honey. Season. Pour this over your broccoli mix to serve.

Nutrition:

226 Calories 7g Protein 12g Fat

30. Tomato Salad

Preparation Time: 22 minutes

Cooking Time: 0 minute

Serving: 4

Size/ portion: 2 cups

Ingredients:

- 1 cucumber, sliced
- ¼ cup sun dried tomatoes, chopped
- 1 lb. tomatoes, cubed
- ½ cup black olives
- 1 red onion, sliced 1 tablespoon balsamic vinegar
- ¼ cup parsley, fresh & chopped 2 tablespoons olive oil

Directions:

1. Get out a bowl and combine all of your vegetables together. To make your dressing mix all your seasoning, olive oil and vinegar.

2. Toss with your salad and serve fresh.

Nutrition:

126 Calories

2.1g Protein

9.2g Fat

31. Wedge Salad with Creamy Blue Cheese Dressing

Preparation time: 15 minutes

Cooking time: 0 minutes

Servings: 4

Ingredients:

- 1 cup nonfat plain Greek yogurt
- Juice of ½ large lemon
- ¼ teaspoon freshly ground black pepper
- ¼ teaspoon salt 1/3 cup crumbled blue cheese
- 2 heads romaine lettuce, stem end trimmed, halved lengthwise
- 1 cup grape tomatoes, halved ½ cup slivered almonds

Directions:

1. Mix the yogurt, lemon juice, pepper, salt, and cheese in a small bowl. Store the dressing in 4 condiment cups. Divide the lettuce halves and tomatoes among 4 large storage containers. Store the almonds separately.

2. To serve, arrange a half-head of romaine on a plate and top with the tomatoes. Sprinkle with 2 tablespoons of almonds and drizzle with the dressing.

Nutrition:

Calories: 216g

Fat: 11g

Carbohydrates: 20g

Fiber: 9g

Protein: 16g

Sodium: 329mg

Dessert Recipes

32. After Meal Apples

Preparation Time: 15 minutes

Cooking Time: 25 minutes

Servings: 2

Size/ Portion: 1 piece

Ingredients:

- Apple, 1 whole, cut into chunks
- Pineapple chunks, ½ cups
- Grapes, seedless, ½ cup
- Orange juice, ¼ cup
- Cinnamon, ¼ teaspoon

Directions:

1. Preheat the oven to 350 °F.
2. Add all the fruits to a baking dish.
3. Drizzle with the orange juice and sprinkle with cinnamon.

4. Bake for 25 minutes, and serve hot.

Nutrition:

124 Calories

3.2g Fat

0.8g Protein

Lunch

33. Purple Potato Soup

Preparation time: 10 minutes

Cooking time: 1 hour and 15 minutes

Servings: 6

Ingredients:

- 6 purple potatoes, chopped
- 1 cauliflower head, florets separated
- Black pepper to the taste
- 4 garlic cloves, minced
- 1 yellow onion, chopped
- 3 tablespoons olive oil
- 1 tablespoon thyme, chopped
- 1 leek, chopped
- 2 shallots, chopped

- 4 cups chicken stock, low-sodium

Directions:

1. In a baking dish, mix potatoes with onion, cauliflower, garlic, pepper, thyme, and half of the oil, toss to coat, introduce in the oven and bake for 45 minutes at 400 °F.
2. Heat a pot with the rest of the oil over medium-high heat, add leeks and shallots, stir and cook for 10 minutes.
3. Add roasted veggies and stock, stir, bring to a boil, cook for 20 minutes, transfer soup to your food processor, blend well, divide into bowls, and serve.

Nutrition:

Calories: 70

Carbs: 15g

Fat: 0g

Protein: 2g

Sodium 6 mg

Dinner

34. Lime Shrimp and Kale

Preparation time: 10 minutes

Cooking time: 20 minutes

Servings: 4

Ingredients:

- 1-pound shrimp, peeled and deveined
- 4 scallions, chopped
- 1 teaspoon sweet paprika 1 tablespoon olive oil
- Juice of 1 lime Zest of 1 lime, grated
- A pinch of salt and black pepper
- 2 tablespoons parsley, chopped

Directions:

1. Bring the pan to medium heat, add the scallions and sauté for 5 minutes. Add the shrimp and the other ingredients, toss, cook

over medium heat for 15 minutes more, divide into bowls and serve.

Nutrition:

Calories: 149

Carbs: 12g

Fat: 4g

Protein: 21g

Sodium: 250 mg

Mains

35. Vegetable Noodles with Bolognese

Preparation time: 15 minutes

Cooking time: 15 minutes

Servings: 4

Ingredients:

- 1.5 kg of small zucchini (e.g., green and yellow)
- 600g of carrots
- 1 onion
- 1 tbsp olive oil
- 250g of beef steak
- Pinch of Salt and pepper
- 2 tablespoons tomato paste
- 1 tbsp flour
- 1 teaspoon vegetable broth (instant)

- 40g pecorino or parmesan
- 1 small potty of basil

Directions:

1. Clean and peel zucchini and carrots and wash. Using a sharp, long knife, cut first into thin slices, then into long, fine strips. Clean or peel the soup greens, wash and cut into tiny cubes. Peel the onion and chop finely. Heat the Bolognese oil in a large pan. Fry hack in it crumbly. Season with salt and pepper.

2. Briefly sauté the prepared vegetable and onion cubes. Stir in tomato paste. Dust the flour, sweat briefly. Pour in 400 ml of water and stir in the vegetable stock. Boil everything, simmer for 7-8 minutes.

3. Meanwhile, cook the vegetable strips in plenty of salted water for 3-5 minutes. Drain, collecting some cooking water. Add the vegetable strips to the pan and mix well. If the sauce is not liquid enough, stir in some vegetable cooking water and season everything again.

4. Slicing cheese into fine shavings. Wash the basil, shake dry, peel off the leaves, and cut roughly. Arrange vegetable noodles, sprinkle with parmesan and basil

Nutrition:

Calories 269

Fat 9.7g

Protein 25.6g

Sodium 253mg

Carbohydrate 21.7g

36. Harissa Bolognese with Vegetable Noodles

Preparation time: 15 minutes

Cooking time: 30 minutes

Servings: 4

Ingredients:

- 2 onions
- 1 clove of garlic
- 3-4 tbsp oil
- 400g ground beef
- Pinch salt, pepper, cinnamon
- 1 tsp Harissa (Arabic seasoning paste, tube)
- 1 tablespoon tomato paste 2 sweet potatoes
- 2 medium Zucchini
- 3 stems/basil
- 100g of feta

Directions:

1. Peel onions and garlic, finely dice. Warm-up 1 tbsp of oil in a wide saucepan. Fry hack in it crumbly. Fry onions and garlic for a short time. Season with salt, pepper, and ½ teaspoon cinnamon. Stir in harissa and tomato paste.

2. Add tomatoes and 200 ml of water, bring to the boil and simmer for about 15 minutes with occasional stirring. Peel sweet potatoes and zucchini or clean and wash. Cut vegetables into spaghetti with a spiral cutter.

3. Warm-up 2-3 tablespoons of oil in a large pan. Braise sweet potato spaghetti in it for about 3 minutes. Add the zucchini spaghetti and continue to simmer for 3-4 minutes while turning.

4. Season with salt and pepper. Wash the basil, shake dry and peel off the leaves. Garnish vegetable spaghetti and Bolognese on plates. Feta crumbles over. Sprinkle with basil.

Nutrition:

Calories 452 Fat 22.3g Protein 37.1g Sodium 253mg Carbohydrate 27.6g

Fish

37. Steamed Tilapia with Green Chutney

Preparation time: 15 minutes

Cooking time: 10 minutes

Servings: 3

Ingredients:

- 1-pound tilapia fillets, divided into 3
- ½ cup green commercial chutney

Directions:

1. Cut 3 pieces of 15-inch lengths foil. In one foil, place one filet in the middle and 1/3 of chutney. Fold over the foil and seal the filet inside. Repeat process for remaining fish. Put packet on the trivet. Steam for 10 minutes. Serve and enjoy.

Nutrition:

Calories: 151.5 Carbs: 1.1g Protein: 30.7g Fats: 2.7g Sodium: 79mg

38. Creamy Haddock with Kale

Preparation time: 15 minutes

Cooking time: 10 minutes

Servings: 5

Ingredients:

- 1 tbsp olive oil
- 1 onion, chopped
- 2 cloves of garlic, minced
- 2 cups chicken broth
- 1 teaspoon crushed red pepper flakes
- 1-pound wild Haddock fillets
- ½ cup heavy cream
- 1 tablespoon basil
- 1 cup kale leaves, chopped
- Pepper to taste

Directions:

1. Place a pot on medium-high fire within 3 minutes. Put oil, then sauté the onion and garlic for 5 minutes. Put the rest of the fixing, except for basil, and mix well. Boil on lower fire within 5 minutes. Serve with a sprinkle of basil.

Nutrition:

Calories: 130.5

Carbs: 5.5g

Protein: 35.7g

Fats: 14.5g

Sodium: 278mg

Poultry

39. Honey Crusted Chicken

Preparation time: 10 minutes

Cooking time: 25 minutes

Servings: 2

Ingredients:

- 1 teaspoon paprika
- 8 saltine crackers, 2 inches square
- 2 chicken breasts, each 4 ounces
- 4 tsp honey

Directions:

1. Set the oven to heat at 375 °F. Grease a baking dish with cooking oil. Smash the crackers in a Ziplock bag and toss them with paprika in a bowl. Brush chicken with honey and add it to the crackers.

2. Mix well and transfer the chicken to the baking dish. Bake the chicken for 25 minutes until golden brown. Serve.

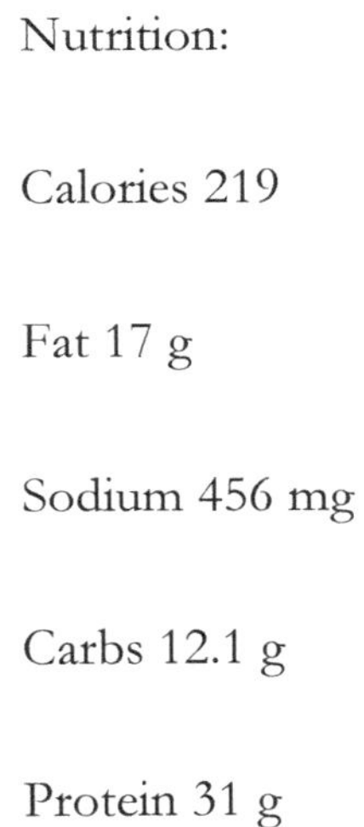

Nutrition:

Calories 219

Fat 17 g

Sodium 456 mg

Carbs 12.1 g

Protein 31 g

40. Paella with Chicken, Leeks, and Tarragon

Preparation time: 10 minutes

Cooking time: 20 minutes

Servings: 2

Ingredients:

- 1 teaspoon extra-virgin olive oil
- 1 small onion, sliced
- 2 leeks (whites only), thinly sliced
- 3 garlic cloves, minced
- 1-pound boneless, skinless chicken breast, cut into strips 1/2-inch-wide and 2 inches long
- 2 large tomatoes, chopped
- 1 red pepper, sliced
- 2/3 cup long-grain brown rice
- 1 teaspoon tarragon, or to taste

- 2 cups fat-free, unsalted chicken broth
- 1 cup frozen peas
- 1/4 cup chopped fresh parsley
- 1 lemon, cut into 4 wedges

Directions:

1. Preheat a nonstick pan with olive oil over medium heat. Toss in leeks, onions, chicken strips, and garlic. Sauté for 5 minutes. Stir in red pepper slices and tomatoes. Stir and cook for 5 minutes.
2. Add tarragon, broth, and rice. Let it boil, then reduce the heat to a simmer. Continue cooking for 10 minutes, then add peas and continue cooking until the liquid is thoroughly cooked. Garnish with parsley and lemon. Serve.

Nutrition:

Calories 388 Fat 15.2 g

Sodium 572 mg Carbs 5.4 g

Protein 27 g

Conclusion

Congrats! Making this far on your MEDITERRANEAN-journey and embracing the MEDITERRANEAN diet as its best!

MEDITERRANEAN Diet has gained popularity in the past few years as it is beneficial in strengthening metabolism and controlling hypertension. Contrary to the popular belief that while following the MEDITERRANEAN diet, one gets to eat vegetarian foods while getting a balanced diet that includes fresh fruits, vegetables, nuts, low-fat dairy products, and whole grains. You do not have to cut down on meat; instead, you have to reduce sodium and fat content from your everyday diet.

The diet also has many health benefits as it helps reduce hypertension and obesity, lower osteoporosis, and prevent cancer. This well-balanced diet strengthens metabolism, which further helps in decomposing the fat deposits stored in the body. As a result, it improves and enhance the overall health of a person.

This cookbook has provided you different MEDITERRANEAN meals from breakfast, lunch, dinner, mains, side dishes, fish and seafood, poultry, vegetables, soups, salads, snacks, and desserts. However, you can consult experts if you suffer from current health conditions or follow certain exercise routines, as this will help you customize the diet as per your requirement.

This diet is easy to follow as you get to everything but in a healthier fashion and limited quantity. Talking about the MEDITERRANEAN diet outside the theory and more in practice reveals its efficiency as a diet. Besides excess research and experiments, the real reasons for people looking into this diet are its specific features. It gives the feeling of ease and convenience, making the users more comfortable with its rules and regulations.

Here are the following reasons why the MEDITERRANEAN Diet works amazingly:

Easy to Adopt: The broad range of options available under the MEDITERRANEAN diet label makes it more flexible for all. It is the reason that people find it easier to switch to and harness its real health benefits. It makes adaptability easier for its users.

Promotes Exercise: It is most effective than all the other factors because not only does it focus on the food and its intake, but it also duly stresses daily exercises and routine physical activities. It is the reason that it produces quick, visible results.

All-Inclusive: With a few limitations, this diet has taken every food item into its fold with certain modifications. It rightly guides about the Dos and Don'ts of all the ingredients and prevents us from consuming those harmful to the body and its health.

CPSIA information can be obtained
at www.ICGtesting.com
Printed in the USA
BVHW041351200421
605393BV00001B/131